EXTREME COOKING

For real men with a stomach of iron and a will to match!

Impress dinner guests with your culinary prowess while maintaining an air of unfailing machismo with this EXTREME COOKING book.

Containing rough-and-ready, occasionally gross, yet remarkably easy-to-follow recipes.

A truly macho approach to cooking.

Managing Editor: Simon Melhuish

Series Editor: Nikole G Bamford

Designer: Stephen Godson

Cover: Radio

Published by

The Lagoon Group

PO Box 311, KT2 5QW, UK

PO Box 990676, Boston, MA 02199, USA

ISBN: 190543930X

© LAGOON BOOKS 2005

www.thelagoongroup.com

Printed in China

EXTREME COOKING

Difficulty Ratings

perfect for beginners

a bit more advanced

could get messy

don't try this at home

EXTREMELY ALCOHOLIC

BOURBON MARINADE FOR STEAK

6 tbs olive oil
4 tbs Dijon mustard
1/2 cup bourbon whiskey
2/3 cup soy sauce
4 tbs red wine vinegar
2 tbs Worcestershire sauce
1/2 cup light or dark brown sugar
4 tbs minced red onion
2 tbs minced garlic
2 tbs minced fresh ginger (optional)
2 tbs salt
4 tsp freshly ground black pepper

Combine the marinade in a small sauce pan. Bring to the boil. Reduce heat and simmer, uncovered, for 15 minutes. Set aside to cool completely.

Trim and score all sides of the meat. Pierce it all over with a sharp knife or skewer and place in a shallow baking dish or ziplock bag. Pour marinade over it and refrigerate overnight. Turn meat occasionally.

Grill or bake as desired.

a bit more advanced

PRAWNS SAMBUCA RECIPE

4 oz olive oil
1 tbs fresh garlic (chopped)
1 tbs fresh shallots (chopped)
16 fresh prawns
1/3 cup dry white wine
1/4 cup Sambuca liqueur
1/4 cup fresh tomato (diced)
1 tbs fresh tarragon (finely chopped)
2 tsp salt and pepper
1/2 cup sweetened butter
2 cups of cooked angel hair pasta
Fresh tarragon leaves
2 chives

Heat oil in a pan, add the garlic, shallots and prawns. Cook for 1 or 2 minutes. Add the wine and Sambuca. Flambé - ignite it and let it flame for 1 minute.

Add tomatoes, tarragon, salt and pepper and cook for 2 more minutes. Add butter and reduce.

Place over individual servings of pasta. Garnish with tarragon leaves and chives.

Serves 4

a bit more advanced

BEER SHRIMP

1 lb/450g raw shrimp
1 1/4 cups beer
1 onion
8 black peppercorns
4 whole cloves
1/2 tsp celery salt

Rinse the shrimp in cold water. Pour the beer into a large stewing pot. Bring beer to a boil. Add everything except the shrimp. Reduce heat and simmer for 5 minutes. Add the shrimp, turning the heat down to medium. Boil the shrimp for 8 minutes.

Peel the shrimp and serve.

perfect for beginners

WHISKEY PASTA

2/3 cup pasta
1/3 cup smoked salmon
1 1/4 cups cream
2 cloves of garlic
3 tsp butter
1 small chopped onion
Salt and pepper
Parmesan cheese
Malt whiskey

Heat the garlic with the cream until they are soft. Remove the garlic and put the cream on a low fire. Fry the onions and add the cream. Let the cream thicken in and add a bit salt and pepper. Finally add a bit of malt whiskey, preferably a smoky one to match the salmon.

Meanwhile, cook the pasta with a bit of salt. When the pasta is done, add the sliced salmon to the sauce and put the sauce over the pasta. Sprinkle the Parmesan cheese over the pasta.

Serves 2

a bit more advanced

TURKEY CHILI WITH BEER

1 large yellow onion (chopped)
6 garlic cloves (minced)
2 tbs cumin seed
6 tbs olive oil
2 red bell peppers (seeded & chopped)
2 polano peppers (seeded & chopped)
2 jalapenos (seeded & chopped)
2 serranos (seeded & chopped)
1 cup red chili paste
3 tbs red chili powder
1 tbs ground cilantro/coriander
1 tbs cinnamon
1 tbs ground black pepper
2lbs/900g ground turkey
4 cups tomatoes with juice (chopped)
2 cups chicken stock
1 cup Mexican beer
7/8 cup Chipotle peppers (usually sold canned in Adobo sauce)
1/4 cup grated unsweetened chocolate

GARNISH
Chopped green onion
Cilantro/coriander
Cheese - grated
Fried tortilla strips
Sour cream

Sauté the onion, garlic and cumin in 3 tbs olive oil until transparent.

Add the chopped peppers and sauté over medium heat for about 10 minutes. Add the chili paste, chili powder, coriander, cinnamon and pepper.

Sauté for 5 minutes and set aside. Brown the turkey in the remaining olive oil. Add the tomatoes, chicken stock, beer and chipotles. Simmer slowly for 30 to 45 minutes. Just before serving, stir in the chocolate. Garnish with chopped green onions, cilantro/coriander, grated cheese, tortilla strips and sour cream.

Serves 8-10

could get messy

BEER BATTER

2 cups flour
1 1/2 tsp baking powder
1 tsp salt
1/2 tsp pepper
2 eggs
1 1/2 cups beer

Mix all the ingredients in a large bowl; beat until smooth.
Coat your fish, vegetables and onion rings liberally in the
batter and fry in at least 3 inches of oil.

perfect for beginners

BOURBON CORN CHOWDER

4 tbs unsalted butter
1 small onion (diced)
2 1/2 cups canned creamed corn
1/4 cup bourbon
1/4 tsp freshly grated nutmeg
1 tsp salt
Freshly ground black pepper
2 to 3 drops hot red pepper sauce
1/2 cup chicken stock
1/2 cup heavy cream

In a small saucepan, melt the butter over medium heat. Add the onion and stir for 5 minutes. Add the corn.

In a small saucepan, heat the bourbon. Ignite it and let it flame for 1 minute. Pour the bourbon, still flaming, over the corn mixture. Stir in the remaining. Heat through.

Serves 4

a bit more advanced

BEER CHEESE

**2lbs/900g mature Cheddar cheese
(leave to stand at room temperature)
2 cloves garlic (crushed)
3 tbs Worcestershire sauce
1 tsp dry mustard
Tabasco to taste
1/2 bottle beer
1 tsp salt**

Cut the cheese into cubes and place them in a food processor or electric mixer. Process until perfectly smooth. Add the garlic, Worcestershire sauce, mustard and tabasco. Blend well. Add the beer, a little at a time, while continuing to beat the cheese, until the mixture is a good, firm spreading consistency. Too much beer will make the cheese too fluffy. Stir in the salt and refrigerate. This keeps very well. Serve on small slices of rye or pumpernickel bread and a glass of cold beer.

Serves 15 to 20

perfect for beginners

CHAMPAGNE CHICKEN

3 skinless boneless chicken breasts
2 tbs butter
1/2 cup heavy cream
Salt and freshly ground pepper
6 thin slices prosciutto
1 tbs butter or margarine
2 tbs olive oil
1/4 cup Champagne (dry)
3 tbs fresh tarragon (1 tbs if dry)

Cut chicken into 1/4in or 1/2cm slices. Melt the butter
and olive oil in a large heavy skillet. Sauté the chicken for
4 to 5 minutes. Remove the chicken and keep warm.
Deglaze the pan with the champagne. Add the cream to
the pan. Add the tarragon and reduce the sauce for two
minutes. Put the chicken back into the pan and bring
to a bare simmer.

Serve on a warm platter with pasta and steamed
vegetables.

Serves 2 to 3

a bit more advanced

MARGARITA WINGS RECIPE

2 lbs/900g chicken wings
1/2 cup gold tequila or mescal
1/4 cup frozen orange juice concentrate
Grated zest of 1 lemon
Juice of 1 lemon
2 cloves garlic (minced)
1/2 tsp ground cumin
1 tsp freshly ground coarse black pepper
1 tsp salt
2 tbs minced cilantro/coriander

Wash the wings, pat dry and place in a ziplock bag.

In a small bowl, combine the remaining ingredients and pour the marinade over the wings in the bag. Seal the bag and refrigerate several hours or overnight.

Prepare a medium-hot charcoal fire or pre-heat a gas grill to medium-high. Drain the wings, discarding the marinade.

Grill the wings, turning often, until they are slightly charred and cooked through, about 25 minutes.

Serves 4

a bit more advanced

perfect for beginners

CHAMPAGNE OYSTERS

12 fresh oysters (opened, juice reserved)
1/4 cup butter
2 shallots (finely chopped)
2 tsp freshly chopped tarragon
1 1/4 cups pink champagne
Salt and black pepper

Melt half the butter in a pan, add the shallots and sauté for 1 minute.

Add the champagne and any oyster juices, chopped tarragon, salt and pepper. Stir well and cook for 2 to 3 minutes.

Remove the oysters from their shells (keeping the shells for later) and add to the pan. Cook over a low heat, stirring for 3 to 4 minutes until cooked through.

Using tongs or a slotted spoon, transfer the oysters back to their individual shells and keep warm. Increase the heat under the pan and whisk the remaining butter into the sauce, a little at a time.

To serve - place the oysters in their shells on individual plates and pour the sauce over the oysters. Serve immediately as a starter.

Serves 4

HOT STUFF

BUZZARD'S BREATH BARBECUE SAUCE

2 cups chopped onions
1 cup very strong coffee
1 cup Worcestershire sauce
1 cup ketchup
1/2 cup cider vinegar
1/2 cup brown sugar
3 tbs chili powder
1 puréed habanero pepper - include seeds
4 garlic cloves (pressed)
1 tsp pepper (freshly ground)

Combine all ingredients in a sauce pan and simmer for 15 minutes. Purée in a blender or food processor.

Use the sauce to baste whatever meat you like. Put leftover sauce in a sterilized jar and refrigerate when cool.

a bit more advanced

could get messy

WICKEDLY HOT WINGS

2 lbs/900g chicken wings
6 whole serrano chili peppers
6 whole red chili peppers
10 whole jalapeno peppers
Large dash of white wine
1 bottle Tabasco sauce
1/2 bottle Worcestershire sauce
10 tbs cayenne pepper
10 tbs cajun sauce
1 tbs salt
3 tbs pepper
1/2 cup vinegar
1/4 cup sugar

In a blender, carefully purée the peppers, wine, vinegar and all the spices. Put the purée into a bowl and marinate the wings in a bowl in the fridge for 5 days.

After 5 days, carefully remove the wings and broil them until cooked. Usually approx 15 mins. Take the marinade, put it on the stove, add 1/4 cup sugar and heat to a boil. Reduce until thick.

Pour over the wings and re-broil for about 5 more minutes. Drink soda water to maximise heat on the tongue but have some cold milk handy to soothe those tastebuds.

WARNING: The fumes are toxic — wear rubber gloves or your fingers will burn!

FLAMING GOOD

FLAMING FISH

4 (8oz/227g) trout fillets

LEMON ONION BASTE:
1/2 cup lemon juice
1/4 tsp salt
1/4 cup salad oil
1/4 tsp sugar
1/8 cup green onions
Dash of pepper
1/3 cup rum (or cognac)

HERBS
Rosemary, fennel, dill, parsley, thyme, sage

Mix the ingredients of the lemon-onion baste.

Grill fillets over a medium heat basting twice on each side with the lemon-onion mixture. Cook 5 to 8 minutes on each side, turning once.

Cover a hot plate with the herbs and place on it the fillets from grill. Sprinkle herbs on top of the fillets. Pour the rum over it and ignite. Try this out-of-doors once before you try it out at a dinner party.

Serve with rice and vegetables or the following flaming salad recipe for fire overkill.

Serves 4

SPINACH SALAD FLAMBÉ

**6 bunches spinach - washed and dried
(1 3/4 cups each bunch)
6 hard-boiled eggs (sliced)
1/4 tsp salt
1/2 tsp ground pepper
12 strips bacon (crisply fried and chopped)
3/4 cup bacon drippings
1/2 cup malt vinegar
1/4 cup lemon juice
4 tsp sugar
1 tsp Worcestershire sauce
1 1/2 oz brandy**

Tear spinach into small pieces and place in a large salad bowl. Add egg slices, salt and pepper.

Mix remaining ingredients except brandy in a small saucepan and heat until very hot. Heat brandy briefly and separately, add to the saucepan and ignite. Pour flaming dressing over spinach and toss gently but thoroughly. Serve on warm salad plates.

Serves 6

a bit more advanced

perfect for beginners

CRAZY COOKING

SCRAPPLE

1/2 hog's head
1 hog's liver
1 hog's heart
1 hog's sweetbreads
Cornmeal (yellow)
Buckwheat flour
Salt & pepper
Sage (dried)
Mace

Separate one hog's head into halves. Take out the eyes and brains. Scrape and thoroughly clean the head. Put 1/2 of the head, along with the liver, heart and sweetbreads of the hog into a large kettle and cover with 4 or 5 quarts of cold water. Simmer gently for 2 or 3 hours, or until the meat falls from the bones. Skim off grease carefully from the surface; remove meat, chop fine and weigh the meat.

For every 3lbs of meat, use 2lbs of meal (2 parts cornmeal and 1 part buckwheat flour) or for every kg of meat use 2/3kg of meal. Add 2 tsp salt, 1/2 tsp pepper, 1 tsp sage and 1 tsp mace. Cook slowly over a low flame about 1 hour. Pour into a pan and let it stand until cold. Cut into slices and fry until golden brown.

GREEN SALAD

1 large package of lime Jell-O
2 cups of hot water
1 cup of cold water
2 tsp of vinegar
2 tsp of salt
Dash of cayenne pepper
2 cups of cottage cheese
1 cup of mayonnaise
1 large can of crushed pineapple

Dissolve Jell-O in hot water. Add cold water and vinegar; stir. Add the cayenne pepper and salt. Stir till it is all dissolved. Chill until slightly thickened. Whip with a beater until fluffy and light. Mix in the cottage cheese and mayonnaise. Drain the pineapple and fold into the Jell-O mixture. Chill until firm.

Serves 4

could get messy

a bit more advanced

CROCODILE SCHNITZELS

8oz/250g crocodile fillets (thinly sliced)
1/2 cup minced walnuts
1 cup each of breadcrumbs, flour, milk, egg

Dust with flour. Dip in egg wash (1 egg beaten with 1 cup milk). Blend walnuts and breadcrumbs and coat crocodile with this mixture. Fry in a preheated mixture of oil and butter. Serve with Tropical Fruit Sauce.

TROPICAL FRUIT SAUCE
1 large mango (diced)
1 papaya (diced)
3 tbsp brown sugar
3 tbsp butter
3 tbsp chopped walnuts
1 tbs rum, brandy or whiskey (optional)
1 cup water

Melt butter in a pan and sauté the walnuts. Add sugar and stir for 2 minutes. Add the mango and papaya and mash. Add water and stir occasionally until the mixture boils. Stir in the spirits, reduce heat and simmer for 15 minutes.

could get messy

could get messy

COW UDDER ECLAIRS

12 fresh lean cow udders
1 pint of whipping cream
1 cup of brown sugar
1 can artichoke hearts
1 stick butter
1 small filleted smelt
1 container of hair removal cream

Soak the cow udders in hair removal cream to remove the hair. Repeat several times if necessary until all hair is removed. Rinse in warm water.

Place a stick of butter into a warm frying pan. Wait until all of the butter has melted, then add the cow udders. Fry them for 15-20 minutes until golden brown.

Chop the artichoke hearts and smelt on a cutting board into fine pieces. In a large bowl, add the whipping cream, brown sugar, chopped artichokes and smelt.

With a mixer on low, whip until creamy. Remove the udders from the pan and make a long slice down the side of each udder. Spread the pudding mixture into each slit. Serve warm or cold.

SLUG FRITTERS

10 freshly killed slugs cleaned of all outer mucus
1/2 cup of cornmeal
1/2 cup of high protein flour
3 eggs
2 extra egg yolks
1/4 cup of heavy cream
4 tbs of butter
4 tsp of sour cream

First chop the slugs into fine mince, then beat the eggs and egg yolks with the heavy cream together. Add the slug mince. Sift the dry ingredients and then cut 2 tbs of butter into that mixture. Add the egg and cream mixture to this and whisk vigorously for one to two minutes. Melt one tbs of butter in a sauté pan and pour the batter into 2 1/2in/7cm cakes in two batches. Fry the little cakes until golden brown. Serve warm with a dollop of sour cream.

Serves 4

don't try this at home

don't try this at home

IGUANA SOUP

1 iguana
1 1/2 quarts of iguana broth
(or chicken broth)
2 chicken bouillon cubes
1 clove of garlic
1 leek
1 tomato, coarsely chopped
1 onion, studded with 3 cloves
1 green pepper, quartered
1/4 small cabbage
1 tsp cumin
1 dash nutmeg
Salt and pepper
1/4 cup vermicelli

Kill, clean, skin and cut the iguana into serving pieces. Or find a specialist shop. Prepare the chicken broth in a heavy kettle adding the garlic, leek, tomato, onion, green pepper and cabbage. Bring to a boil, reduce heat and simmer for 30 minutes. Add the iguana and simmer an additional half hour, or until the meat is tender. Remove from the fire. Strain broth, discarding vegetables. Bone the iguana and set the meat aside.

Return the broth to the fire and add cumin, nutmeg, vermicelli and salt and pepper. Simmer for about five minutes until the vermicelli is tender. Add the iguana and heat thoroughly. Serve piping hot.
Serves 6

LIZARD TONGUES ON CRACKERS

1 cup lizard tongues
1 cup grated cheese
1/4 cup red caviar
1/4 cup parsley
Tabasco sauce
Worcestershire sauce
Ritz crackers

Spread the crackers on a greased baking dish. Top with cheese and lizard tongues. Sprinkle a little parsley on top and a drop or two of Tabasco and Worcestershire sauce. Bake for 10 minutes at 325F/170C. Remove from oven and top with red caviar.

don't try this at home

don't try this at home

SPIDER SALAD

Arachnids have a very delicate flavor and should not be overcooked. Use whatever spiders that are rife in your part of the world but beware of the poisonous varieties like Black Widows.

Steam your spiders live, as this is a safe method of both asphyxiating them and keeping them crisp and fresh. Chop the legs off the larger spiders and quarter them. Prepare a bed of lettuce, parsley, chopped mushrooms, radishes and scallions. Toss in approximately 1 cup chopped spiders.Dress with olive oil, vinegar, lemon juice and fresh ground pepper. Or serve with this great dressing.

BEER SALAD DRESSING
1/2 cup olive oil
Fresh ground black pepper
3 tbsp wine vinegar to taste
1/4 cup beer
Dash garlic powder
3/4 tsp sea salt (regular salt will do)

Beat or shake all together. Delicious when used with potato salad, coleslaw, pasta or spider salads.

COCKENTRICE (A Medieval Marvel)

1 suckling pig, about 7lbs/3kg
1 large roasting chicken, about 6lbs/2 1/2 kg
6 egg yolks
1/4 tsp powdered saffron
1/2 cup all-purpose flour
1/4 cup white wine
1 tbs fresh parsley leaves
(very finely chopped)
1 tbs flour

The extraordinary beasts created by this recipe were never real. A chicken and pork visual and edible feast was intended to startle a medieval audience as well as feed. It was the job of the medieval cook to create extravagant illusions and push the boundaries of culinary artistry.

Bake the chicken and the suckling pig separately at 375F/190C until tender; the chicken ought to take 2 hours, the suckling pig closer to 3.

Cut the chicken in half with the incision running around the body behind the wings. The forward half is thus separated from the hind parts. Similarly cleave the pig so that the head and shoulders are cut from the back half of the animal. With a strong butcher's thread or similar sew the forward half of the chicken to the back half of the pig; sew the pig's head and shoulders to the back half of the chicken.

Each is now a cockentrice. Turn oven up to 400F/200C.

Lightly beat the egg yolks. Mix in the saffron and flour to make a thick fluid. Paint this on the suture lines as well as various parts of either the "face" or appendages - gold snout and gold nails were typical adornments.

Return these marvelous animals to the oven so the "gilt" may set and the final creatures appear resplendent.

Mix the parsley in white wine with flour until the green color well permeates the fluid. If not a bright green, add two drops of green food coloring. Paint on "feathers" or designs for the final embellishment of the cockentrice.

Serves a whole banqueting hall.

could get messy

CROW CASSEROLE

6 crow breasts
1 quart sauerkraut
6 strips bacon
1/3 cup chopped onions

Brown the crow breasts in a skillet. When browned, place them in a casserole dish on top of a 1 1/2 in/4cm layer of sauerkraut.

Lay a strip of bacon on each breast and sprinkle the onion on them. Next layer over them again the sauerkraut and some of its juices.

Bake at 350F/180C for 2 hrs.

Serves 3 to 4

don't try this at home

TILLER RATTLESNAKE SURPRISE

1 rattlesnake
1/4 cup melted butter
1 tsp garlic salt

Find one full grown rattlesnake and kill it. Remove its
head and rattle, being sure not to break any
of the capsules because they can be harmful.
(CAUTION: a snake can still bite, even when dead.
Skin it, clean it, & remove entrails. Cut into finger-long
portions. Alternatively find a specialist butcher to
prepare the snake for you.

Put snake pieces, melted butter and garlic salt together
in a tin foil packet. Put packet on an open flame, letting
the snake boil in the butter for 7 to 8 minutes. Remove
packet from the flame and let cool for 2 minutes.

Remove the snake from the packet, peel the meat from
the bones and eat!

don't try this at home

TUNA TWINKIE SOUFFLÉ

1 tbs rendered chicken fat (divided)
12 Hostess Twinkies
Salt and white pepper
1/2 tsp dry mustard
4 eggs (separated)
2 cans tuna in oil (drained/reserve oil)

Preheat oven to 350F/180C. Grease a 7in/18cm soufflé dish with 1 tsp of chicken fat and 1 tsp tuna oil.

Slice Twinkies in half lengthwise. Remove and reserve cream filling. In a large food processor, combine the Twinkie cakes, half of the Twinkie filling and the remaining chicken fat and tuna oil. Blend until the mixture has reached the consistency of a thin batter.

Transfer to a medium saucepan and cook over low heat. Stir in salt, white pepper and mustard. Remove from the heat.

Beat in egg yolks, one at a time, beating thoroughly after each addition. Fold in the tuna. In a medium bowl, beat the egg whites until stiff but not dry. Fold beaten egg whites into the tuna mixture. Pour into a greased soufflé dish.

Bake in an oven at 350F/180C for 40 to 45 minutes, or until puffed and golden brown. Top with remaining Twinkie cream. Serve with a tossed salad.

BARBECUED QUAIL

1 cup scallions (finely chopped)
1/4 cup honey
2 tbs Worcestershire sauce
4 large cloves of garlic (minced)
1 tbs dry mustard
2 tsp ancho chili powder
1 cup Chablis
Sea salt and fresh ground black peppercorns
4 each 4oz/113g semi-boneless quail

Combine all except the quail and heat in a saucepan for about 15 minutes over a medium heat. Remove from the heat and cool to room temperature.

Place the quail in a baking dish and pour about 2/3 of the sauce over them. Reserve the rest for basting while grilling.

Marinate for about 30 minutes at room temperature and then grill for about 3 to 4 minutes on each side. Remove when the flesh is firm and juices run clear from the leg when pierced. Remember to baste a couple times while grilling. Serve immediately.

could get messy

a bit more advanced

STUFFED SQUID WITH CHOCOLATE SAUCE

1lb/450g squid (cleaned, dried)
1/2lb/225g ground pork
Olive oil
1 onion (finely diced)
1 small carrot (finely diced)
2 garlic cloves (minced)
2 parsley sprigs (minced)
1/4 cup bread crumbs
1/2 cup pine nuts (lightly toasted)
Salt and pepper
1 cup fish, shellfish or chicken stock
1/2 cup dry white wine
10 to 12 almonds (blanched, roasted)
1/8 cup Ibarra brand chocolate, (Mexican)
(coarsely grated)
 2 slices fried crustless French bread

Remove heads and tentacles from squid and set bodies aside. Mince heads and tentacles, then mix well with the ground pork using a food processor.

Heat about 1/2in/1cm of olive oil in a paella pan or large skillet and sauté the onion, carrot, garlic and parsley in it until the onions are wilted; add the pork mixture, crumbs and half the pine nuts, mixing together well and cooking until the meat is well done. Season to taste with salt and pepper, then remove the mixture from the pan and drain on paper towels or in a colander.

Preheat oven to 350F/180C.

When the pork mixture is cool, lightly stuff the reserved squid bodies with it being careful not to overstuff or the squid will shrink and tear during cooking. Bake the squid in a single layer, uncovered, in a lightly oiled baking dish for about 20 minutes.

Meanwhile, deglaze the pan with the stock and wine, simmering until it is reduced by about half. While the liquid reduces, finely grind the almonds, remaining pine nuts, chocolate and fried bread all together; then moisten with a bit of the liquid to make a thick paste (it must be fine, without a grainy texture). Add this mixture to the reduced liquid, stir in well, return to the boil and season to taste. Pour over the stuffed squid, or spoon onto serving plates and set the squid on top of the sauce.

could get messy

CAJUN POSSUM CHILI

Italian-style tomato sauce
Chili powder (as much as you can handle)
1 large possum
5-10 chili peppers
5-10 red bell peppers
5-10 jalapeno peppers
Cayenne pepper
Salt and pepper to taste
Kidney beans

If you've just caught the possum or run it over, skin it and remove all internal organs, head, claws and bones. Or take it to your local butcher to prepare it.

Get a large pot and add enough tomato sauce to cover the possum. Chop all the peppers and add the rest of the ingredients. Warm through. Add the pieces of possum, let rest for a while and then grill pieces for about 20 minutes or until cooked through.

Warning: you will need copius amounts of milk, toilet tissue and air freshener for the aftermath. Pork is an acceptable substitute for possum.

Serves 4-6

don't try this at home

BANANAS FOSTER

4 bananas
6 tbs butter
6 tbs dark brown sugar
1/4 cup strong rum

Peel bananas and carefully slice lengthwise. Melt the butter in a large nonstick skillet. With a large, flat spatula carefully add the banana halves, round side down. Cook over moderate heat for 2 minutes. Being very careful, turn the bananas over to the flat side and sprinkle brown sugar over them. Continue cooking for 2 more minutes. Remove from the heat. Pour rum over the bananas, wait a few seconds then light. Bring to the table flaming. Serve with vanilla ice cream.

a bit more advanced

SNAIL PORRIDGE

SNAIL BUTTER
1/8 cup garlic cloves, peeled
1/6 cup button mushrooms, finely chopped
1/6 cup shallots, finely chopped
7/8 cup butter, at room temperature
2 tbs Dijon mustard
1 1/2 tbs ground almonds
Salt
1 1/2 cups flatleaf parsley, chopped
3 tbs Parma ham
SNAILS
72 cooked snails
1 carrot, peeled and thinly sliced
1 onion, peeled and thinly sliced
1 fennel bulb, finely sliced
1 stick of celery, finely sliced
1/2 cup button mushrooms, finely sliced
2 garlic cloves
Bouquet garni made from bay leaves, thyme
and rosemary
PORRIDGE
1 tbs Parma ham
1 small fennel bulb
1 cup snail cooking stock
4 1/2 tbs porridge oats
5 tbs snail butter
knob of butter
1 tsp sherry
3 tsp walnut oil

For the snail butter, blanch and refresh the garlic three to four times. Heat 3 tbs of the butter in a frying pan and sweat the mushrooms and shallots for 5-10 minutes until softened. Keep to one side. Put the remaining snail butter ingredients in a food processor and purée until smooth. Rub the mix through a fine-meshed sieve, then mix in the Parma ham, mushrooms and shallots. Place the mix on a sheet of cling film and roll into a cylinder. Store in the fridge to harden.

To cook the snails, add them to a pan of boiling water and bring it back to the boil. Skim the surface and reduce the heat so that the water simmers very gently. Add the rest of the ingredients and simmer for three hours, remove from the heat and leave to cool a little before straining through muslin. Reserve the snails.

Finely shred the Parma ham and slice the fennel as thinly as possible. Heat the stock in a saucepan and when it's simmering add the oats. Stir until all of the liquid has been absorbed. Remove from the heat and beat in the snail butter. Season generously. Sauté the snails in butter and drain. To serve, spoon the porridge onto the plates and top with the sliced ham. Top the porridge and ham with the sautéed snails. Toss the fennel with the vinegar and walnut oil and season. Place the fennel on top of the porridge and serve.

Serves 12

don't try this at home

HAGGIS

1 sheep's lungs (optional)
1 sheep's stomach
1 sheep's heart
1 sheep's liver
1 1/2 cups suet
3/4 cups ground oatmeal
3 onions (finely chopped)
1 tsp salt
1/2 tsp freshly ground pepper
1/4 tsp cayenne pepper
1/2 tsp nutmeg
3/4 cup stock

Wash lungs and stomach well, rub with salt and rinse. Remove membranes and excess fat. Soak in cold salted water for several hours. Turn stomach inside out for stuffing.

Cover heart and liver with cold water. Bring to a boil, reduce heat, cover and simmer for 30 minutes. Chop heart and coarsely grate liver. Toast oatmeal in a skillet on top of the stove, stirring frequently, until golden. Combine all and mix well. Loosely pack mixture into stomach, about two thirds full. Remember, oatmeal expands in cooking.

Press any air out of stomach and truss securely. Put into boiling water to cover. Simmer for 3 hours, uncovered, adding more water as needed to maintain water level. Prick stomach several times with a sharp needle when it begins to swell; this keeps the bag from bursting. Place on a hot platter, removing trussing strings. Serve with a spoon.

Serve with nips, neeps and tatties — nips of whiskey, roasted turnips and potatoes.

could get messy

CURRIED KANGAROO TAIL

1 kangaroo tail
1/4 cup butter
1 tbs flour
1 tbs curry powder
2 onions, sliced
1 sour apple diced
1 tbs lemon juice
1 1/2 cups stock
Salt

Wash, blanch and dry the tail thoroughly and divide it at
the joints. Fry the tail lightly in hot butter, take it up, put
in the sliced onions and fry them for a few minutes
without browning. Sprinkle in the flour and curry powder
and cook gently for at least 20 minutes, stirring
frequently. Add the stock, bring to the boil, stirring
meanwhile and replace the tail in the stewpan. Cover
closely and cook gently until tender (from 2 to 3 hours),
then add the lemon juice and more seasoning if
necessary. Arrange the pieces of tail on a hot dish,
strain the sauce over and serve with boiled rice.

could get messy

DESSERTS

PEACHES FLAMED IN BOURBON

6 peaches (peeled and halved)
1 cup bourbon
1/4 cup butter
3/4 cup sugar
1/2 cup peach nectar
Crushed macaroons

Soak peaches in bourbon for 24 hours. Drain and reserve bourbon. Melt butter in a large skillet, add sugar and cook until caramelized. Add peaches, flat side down. Cook until slightly browned, turn and repeat. Heat 1/4 cup of the bourbon and pour over peaches. Ignite. Shake pan until flames die. Pour in peach nectar; heat for a few moments. Place flat side up on serving dish. Sprinkle with crushed macaroons and serve.

Serves 6

a bit more advanced

CHOCOLATE BEER CAKE

FOR THE CAKE
1/4 cup cocoa powder
7/8 cup stout
1/2 cup very soft butter
1 1/4 cups dark soft brown sugar
2 large eggs, beaten
3/4 cups plain flour
1/4 tsp baking powder
1 tsp bicarbonate of soda

You will also need two 8in/20cm sponge tins,
1 1/2in/4cm deep, lightly greased and the bases lined
with baking parchment, also lightly greased.

Pre-heat the oven to 350F/180C. Cream the butter
and sugar together, beating thoroughly for 3 or 4
minutes until pale and fluffy. Now gradually beat in the
eggs, a little at a time, beating well between each
addition. Next, sift the flour, baking powder and
bicarbonate of soda on to a sheet of baking parchment.

Then weigh the cocoa and put it in a separate bowl,
gradually stirring the stout into it. Now carefully and
lightly fold into the egg mixture small quantities of the
sifted flour alternately with the cocoa-stout liquid. Then,
when both have been added, divide the cake mixture
equally between the 2 tins and level it out.

Bake the sponges in the centre of the oven for 30-35 minutes. The cakes should be flat on top and feel springy and will have shrunk slightly from the side of the tin. Leave them to cool in the tins for 5 minutes before turning out on to a wire rack to cool further, carefully stripping off the base papers.

See next page for icing.

could get messy

FOR THE ICING
1/2 cup icing sugar (sifted)
1/4 cup very soft butter
2 tbs stout
1/2 cup dark chocolate
(at least 50% cocoa solids)
4 tbs walnut pieces (finely chopped)

To decorate:
8 walnut halves
cocoa powder for dusting

To make the icing, beat the icing sugar and butter together until blended, then gradually add the stout, making sure it is thoroughly mixed in after each addition. Now melt the chocolate in a bowl set over hot water, making sure the bottom of the bowl doesn't touch the water. Then, when it's melted, remove the bowl from the water and carefully fold the chocolate into the icing mixture. Now remove a third of the icing to a separate bowl and stir in the chopped walnuts.

After all the icing has cooled to a spreadable consistency, sandwich the cake with the walnut icing. Then spread the remaining two-thirds of the icing on top of the cake, using a palette knife. Next, dust the walnut halves with cocoa powder and arrange on top of the cake. Let the icing set and eat!

Serves 8

SPAM SORBET

1 large can of spam
1 packet aspic
2 avocados
2 cups lemon sorbet
2 cornets
Crunchy bacon bits

Blend up spam and aspic until smooth and creamy. Do the same with the avocados. Retrieve your empty large spam can and press Spam mixture into the bottom. Add a layer of the lemon sorbet, then a layer of the avocado paste. Several alternating layers can be added to suit. Pop in the freezer for an hour then scoop onto cones, sprinkle with bacon bits and enjoy.

could get messy

DEEP-FRIED ICE CREAM

2 cups ice cream (any flavor)
1 loaf sliced white bread
6 to 8 cups canola oil, for frying
1/2 cup sugar
2 tsp cinnamon

Place a plate or sheet pan in the freezer and let it chill for at least 1 hour or overnight.

Using a large ice cream scoop, make balls of ice cream and place them on the sheet pan then return them to the freezer.

Cut the crusts off the sliced bread and using about 2 slices per ice cream ball, form the bread around the ice cream using your hands to pack it like a snow ball. Once it's completely covered return it to the freezer.

In a medium saucepan, heat 3 inches of canola oil to 365F/185C. Drop the covered ice cream balls, one at a time, into the hot oil and fry, turning occasionally so they color evenly, until golden brown on all sides.

Remove from oil and briefly drain on paper towels. Stir together the sugar and cinnamon. Coat fried ice cream in the cinnamon sugar mixture. Serve immediately.

HONEY CHERRY CHAMPAGNE SAUCE

2 cups canned tart red cherries
1/4 cup honey
1/4 cup chilled Champagne

Drain the cherries reserving 1/4 cup liquid. Purée the cherries in a blender; add reserved liquid and honey. Bring mixture to the boil in a saucepan; reduce the heat and simmer. Cook about 15 to 20 minutes or until reduced by half; cool. Just before serving, stir in chilled Champagne.

Serve with orange slices or ice cream - delicious.

could get messy

a bit more advanced

AVOCADO ICE CREAM

2 large avocados (peeled, seeded, sliced)
4 cups medium or whipping cream
3 tbs tequila or light rum
3 large egg yolks
2 tbs all-purpose flour
1/4 cup sugar
Pinch of salt
1 1/2 tsp vanilla

Combine the avocados and 1 cup of the cream.
Add the tequila and blend until smooth. Refrigerate
for 2 hours. Beat the egg yolks with another cup of
the cream. In a saucepan, combine the flour, sugar,
and salt and whisk to blend thoroughly. Slowly whisk in
the remaining 2 cups of cream and stir over medium
heat until slightly thickened. Whisk half the hot mixture
into the egg yolks. Pour the mixture back into the pan
and stir over medium heat for 1 minute. Remove from
the heat, stir in the vanilla and chill for 2 hours.
Combine the avocado mixture and the egg yolk
mixture and put in your ice cream machine or freeze.

Serves 8

a bit more advanced

SORBET SHOTS

2 cups sorbet
Melon baller
3/4 cup liqueur (any you like)

Place small scoops of sorbet, using a melon baller, into shot glasses (only 1 flavor per glass).

Top the sorbet with about 1 tbs of matching flavored liqueur.

Serves 10

perfect for beginners

MARGARITA BALLS

1 1/2 cups vanilla wafers
1/2 cup pretzel crumbs
(about 1 cup pretzels)
2 cups confectioners' sugar (sifted)
3/4 cup frozen margarita or limeade
concentrate (thawed)
3/4 cup cream cheese
1 tsp tequila
1 tsp Triple Sec (orange liqueur)
Grated rind from 1 lime
1/4 cup green decorator sugar
1 cup granulated sugar

Crumb the vanilla wafers in a food processor. Do the same with the pretzels. Remove crumbs and reserve. In a large bowl, combine wafer crumbs, pretzel crumbs, powdered sugar, margarita concentrate and cream cheese. Add tequila and Triple Sec, if desired. Stir until well blended. Divide the mixture in half. Wrap each half tightly in plastic wrap and set aside.

Combine half the grated lime with decorator sugar and half with granulated sugar on small saucers or in small bowls, stirring to distribute lime peel evenly. Remove plastic wrap from 1 portion of the dough and shape into small 1in/2.5cm balls. After shaping each ball, roll each in green or white sugar. Work quickly, because the treats dry quickly. Repeat until all dough is used. Store in an airtight container in refrigerator for up to 1 week.

Makes 84 balls

a bit more advanced

FLAMING CHOCOLATE FONDUE RECIPE

1/4 cup milk
1/2 cup milk chocolate
1/4 cup caramel syrup
2 tbs pecans, chopped
2 tbs rum

FOR THE DIPPING BASKET
Fruit (cut)
(strawberries, bananas and pineapple)
Marshmallows
cake (cubed), madeira, fruit or pound cake

Soften milk chocolate in the microwave. Heat the milk in the fondue pot. Once it's hot, add the softened chocolate. Stir until you have a smooth consistency. Pour caramel into a pool in the middle of the chocolate. When it's time to serve, pour the rum over the top of the chocolate. Leave a small amount on the spoon to ignite with a lighter. Use the flaming spoon to ignite the rum on the chocolate. Add the chopped pecans to the chocolate. Allow the flame to burn out.

All dipping items should be skewered and dipped in the chocolate. Be careful as the chocolate tends to be hotter at the sides and bottom.

Serves 2

GARLIC ICE CREAM

3 cups whole milk
1/2 tsp freshly chopped garlic
1 vanilla bean (split in half)
1 cup heavy cream
1 1/2 cups granulated sugar
9 egg yolks

Put the milk, garlic and vanilla in a saucepan. Bring to the boil and remove from the heat.

In a mixing bowl, blend the cream, sugar and egg yolks.

Strain the scalded milk into the egg and sugar mixture, stirring constantly.

Return the combined mixture to the pan and stir continuously over moderate heat until it coats the back of a spoon, about 10-15 minutes.

Cool over a bowl of iced water and freeze until firm.

Serves 4-6

could get messy

a bit more advanced

CRICKET COOKIES

2 1/4 cups flour
1 tsp baking soda
1 tsp salt
1 cup butter (softened)
3/4 cup sugar
3/4 cup brown sugar
1 tsp vanilla
2 eggs
1 1/2 cups chocolate chips
1 cup chopped nuts
1/2 cup dry-roasted crickets

Preheat oven to 375F/190C. In a small bowl combine the flour, baking soda and salt; set aside. In a large bowl combine the butter, sugar, brown sugar and vanilla; beat until creamy. Beat in the eggs. Gradually add the flour mixture and insects, mixing well. Stir in chocolate chips. Drop rounded measuring teaspoonfuls onto an ungreased cookie sheet. Bake for 8-10 minutes.

don't try this at home

DEMENTED DRINKS

GUINNESS FLOAT

1 1/2 cups Guinness stout
3/4 cup chocolate ice cream

Place chocolate ice cream in a pint (20fl oz) glass.

Add Guinness very slowly, taking care that it doesn't foam over the brim.

Drink!

Serves 1

perfect for beginners

TWO FABULOUS SHAKES

SPAM SHAKE

1 can of spam
1 tin of anchovies
4 cups of beer
1/2 cup tomato juice
1 tsp Dijon mustard
1/2 cup chopped up parsley
1/4 cup chopped scallions
Dash of Tabasco
Salt and pepper to taste

Put all the ingredients in a blender and blend until smooth.

Serve chilled with a celery stick.

perfect for beginners

HOT & SOUR SHAKE

**You need hot peppers
(whatever variety you like)
6 cups of lemon juice
1/2 cup of chili sauce or tabasco
1 scoop of vanilla ice cream
cup of milk**

Chop hot peppers before putting in blender.

Deseed them if you don't want your mouth to burn.

Put ingredients in a blender until smooth.

perfect for beginners

SWEDISH GLOGG RECIPE

2 cups fresh orange juice
1/4 cup sliced almonds
3/4 cup golden raisins
1/2 cup pitted whole prunes (cut in half)
8 whole cloves
Small cinnamon sticks (broken in half)
1/2 inch fresh ginger
4 whole cardamom pods, bruised
3 cups bottle ruby port
3/4 cup brandy
3/4 cup vodka or aquavit

Place orange juice, almonds, raisins and prunes into a large pan. Tie cloves, cinnamon, ginger and cardamom in cheesecloth and add to the pan. Bring mixture to a boil, then lower heat and simmer 45 minutes. Discard spice bag and add the port to the pan. Heat until just beginning to simmer, but do not boil. Add the brandy and vodka and heat through.

Carefully ignite mixture with a match (throw the lit match into the mix, quickly step back several feet and wait for flames to subside - make sure nothing nearby will be ignited from the flambé, then cover the pan with a lid to extinguish. Remove match from brew. Serve warm.

Serves 4-5

TWO FANTASTIC SANDWICHES

ICE CREAM SANDWICH

2 slices of white bread
Soft-serve ice cream (any flavour)

Spread the ice cream on one slice and cover with the other slice.

Serves 1

MARS BAR SANDWICH

2 slices of crusty bread
1 Mars Bar

Butter the bread. Cover one slice with a thinly sliced and warmed Mars Bar.

For extra taste add a sour chopped green apple. Cover with a second slice of bread.

Serves 1

a bit more advanced

perfect for beginners

CAMPSITE FAVOURITES

CAMPFIRE CASSEROLE

**3 cups mushroom soup
(or whatever flavour you have to hand)
2 1/2 cups water
2 tsp instant minced onion
3/4 tsp salt
1/4 tsp pepper
3/4 cup dry hash brown potatoes
1 1/2 cups luncheon meat (cubed)
2 cups whole green beans (drain them if
canned)**

In a large skillet, stir soup and water together until smooth. Add seasonings. Stir in remaining. Heat through, stirring frequently, until potatoes are tender.

perfect for beginners

HOT DOGS IN BEER

1 1/2 cups beer
1 lb/450g Frankfurters
Hot dog buns (warmed)
Sauerkraut (warmed)

Put the beer and frankfurters in a casserole dish. Cover it and heat in a microwave oven for 6 to 8 minutes

Serve on hot buns with warmed sauerkraut.

perfect for beginners

SPIDER DOGS

1 hot dog
Boiling water,
1 pot (if making on stove at home)
1 long fork (if making over fire or barbecue)

Slit the ends of a hot dog with an 'X' then place on a fork and cook over a fire or barbecue until the ends curl like a spider.

If making at home on the stove, cut an 'X' in the ends of the hotdog and place in boiling water and wait till the ends curl like a spider.

perfect for beginners